DIY Pensions

A Simple Guide to Pensions, SIPPs and Retirement Planning

By John Edwards

A simple and, I hope, accessible guide to UK pensions including cost effective DIY ways to build a personal pension pot using a low cost SIPP, how to plan for an early retirement, how to use the option of income drawdown in retirement and an overview of the new flat rate state pension.

-----for Juno, Eddie, Stan, Alex & Felix-----

Updated 4th Edition - Copyright © May 2018 John Edwards

Disclaimer

I do not provide personal investment advice and I am not a qualified financial adviser. I am an amateur investor. All information found here, including any ideas, opinions, views, predictions, forecasts, suggestions, or investment selection, expressed or implied herein, are for **informational or educational purposes only and should not be construed as personal investment advice.** While the information provided is believed to be accurate, it may include errors or inaccuracies. Because I am writing for a large audience, I can make no guarantees whatsoever that the information contained in this booklet will be applicable to your individual situation. I encourage you to do your own research before making any financial decision, and to seek out professional advice from an Independent Financial Adviser (IFA) if you are unsure.

Contents

Foreword by Andy Bell

1. Introduction

2. The Basics

3. Types of Pension
3.1 Company Scheme
3.2 Workplace Pension
3.3 Personal Pension
3.4 Stakeholder
3.5 SIPP

4. The State Pension
4.1 Old Pension
4.2 New Flat Rate Pension
4.3 National Insurance Credits
4.4 Changes to the State Pension

5. Personal Pensions
5.1 What is it?
5.2 How much to pay in?
5.3 What Size Pot Do I Need?
5.4 Effect of Delaying the Start
5.5 Tax Relief for High Earners
5.6 Director of Small Limited Company
5.7 Effect of Pension Charges
5.8 Do I Need a Financial Advisor?
5.9 Possibly a Robo Advisor?

6. Planning for Retirement
6.1 Preparing an Outline Plan
6.2 Work Out Your Target Figure
6.3 A Look at Planned Early Retirement
6.4 Pension or Pay Off Mortgage?

7. Building the DIY Pension Pot
7.1 A SIPP Can be the Ideal Option
7.2 Selecting a SIPP Provider
7.3 Asset Allocation & Attitude to Risk
7.4 Passive or Active Investing?
7.5 A Model Passive Portfolio

8. Annuities & Income/Flexi Drawdown
8.1 Annuities overview
8.2 Income / Flexi-Drawdown
8.3 Pension Benefits after 2015
8.4 Pensionwise

9. Managing Income Drawdown
9.1 Sustainable Income Level
9.2 Natural Yield
9.3 Use of Investment Trusts and Shares
9.4 Bonds & Fixed Income
9.5 Sell Off Investments for 'income'
9.6 Safe Withdrawal Rate
9.7 What Level of Drawdown is Sustainable?
9.8 Common Drawdown Methods

10. Pension or ISA?
10.1 Lifetime ISA

11. End bit... and some useful websites

Foreword by Andy Bell

UK-focussed financial books are relatively few compared to their USA counterparts, so I am pleased to provide a few words in support of this short guide which provides the basic ingredients to help the reader build, manage and invest for a more comfortable retirement.

For anyone thinking of starting to save for the long term, this book is well worth a read. The author not only talks the talk but has walked the walk and the book reflects Edwards' experience of building a pension pot and later moving to drawdown. Drawing on this experience, the author provides several practical examples of the nuts and bolts of operating the basic self-invested personal pension.

Edwards whole ethos is to support the diy investor and questions a system in which the small investor stakes all of his hard-earned savings for maybe 30 or 40 years, takes 100% of risk on the market and yet receives just 50% of the market returns (often much less). No one is better placed or have greater incentive than the reader to make the most of their finances.

The book provides lots of useful information and insight into the often complex world of pensions which will help those who are looking to take more responsibility for their future financial security.

Many ordinary people lack confidence when it comes to matters of personal finance and would regard the world of pensions as complex and mysterious. In this book, Edwards shows that for those willing to learn, it is possible for the average person to set up and manage a basic diy sipp and, in the process, save many thousands of pounds in fees.

Andy Bell

Andy Bell is co-founder and CEO of AJ Bell, one of the UK's largest online investment platforms and stockbroker services with over 140,000 customers and assets under administration exceeding £40 billion. AJ Bell were the first to offer execution-only SIPPs to the ordinary retail investor in 2000.

1. Introduction

This guide is a follow-up to my first book **"DIY Introduction to Personal Finance".** The aim of this second book is to collate the knowledge I have accumulated over the past 25 years and bring it all together in one concise format which I hope may be useful for others who are thinking about their longer term savings and pension plans.

For most of this period I have been actively running my own investment portfolios, including my self invested personal pension - sipp. For some 5 years I was working in financial services as a financial adviser and therefore have experience of personal financial issues from both sides of the fence so to speak. I am now retired and therefore have a little more time to write about these matters and pass on some of the knowledge I have gained over the years.

As people get into their 30s and 40s, most know they really should be doing something about savings for retirement but maybe are put off by things they may have read about pension mis-selling scandals or have no confidence in financial advisers not to mention the upfront costs of the advice fees or may just think its too late to do anything worthwhile.

This book is written mainly for the benefit of those who know they need to do something about a pension but are confused about where to start. It is written for those who just keep 'putting it off' to a later time to hopefully spur them on to make a start.

Pensions do not need to be complicated. However a diy approach is not for everyone - much will depend upon temperament and confidence so take a little time to read this guide, read around the subject via some of the links, make a few notes. It will not take long to become familiar with the basics. From there you will hopefully learn whether you have the confidence to take more responsibility for your pension plans and future prosperity.

Well done for getting this far!

Mention the words pension or annuity and many people will glaze over. For younger people it may not be a priority, they may be more focussed on buying a house and/or bringing up a family. Money may be tight and finding a bit more for a pension is just not possible. Further constraints may involve repayment of student loans.

Pensions are possibly one of the most important areas of finances affecting most people and it is therefore essential to understand the basics so that, at the very least, you can make informed decisions about the future.

In the past, the pensions industry has been able to get away with charging far too much and, as a result, consumers have received less pension return than they might reasonably have expected. I hope books like this will show ordinary people that there are other less costly options available.

Hopefully, by the time you have reached the end of this guide you will have a much clearer understanding of the different types of pension, and whether you need to take steps to address your longer term finances - steps towards a more comfortable and possibly earlier retirement.

In April 2016, the government introduced the new flat rate (so called) state pension which started at £155 per week for all new pensioners - except not everyone will qualify for the headline amount. For many people, the state pension will represent a significant percentage of their retirement income and I have therefore included a chapter to explain some of the main changes and provisions.

This updated version also covers the radical changes to pension freedoms which came into force in 2015.

My views on investment strategy have evolved since the publication of the first edition in 2013 and therefore the changes to this edition incorporate and reflect a greater emphasis on low cost index investing.

Without the benefit of any financial education at school, or possibly in many cases, guidance from parents, it can be a daunting prospect when young people are suddenly expected to take such a big decisions as starting a pension or think about longer term financial planning.

I have deliberately tried to keep this guide as simple as possible and to avoid 'jargon' often used by the pensions industry and financial 'experts' who have an interest in maintaining an air of illusion and mystery around this subject.

In the book, there are no fancy tables and graphs - just plain headings and basic information laid out in what I hope is an easy to follow format.

2. The Basics

There are different types of pension - state pension, personal pension and occupational or company pension - are three common types.

This guide mainly relates to **personal pensions**.

A pension is a tax efficient way of saving money for retirement. For every £100 you pay in, the taxman will add a further £25 - more if you are a higher rate tax payer.

You can save as much as you earn in a pension, however....

Tax relief on contributions is currently capped at £40,000 per year.

You cannot build up a pension pot of more than £1 million over your lifetime.

You can have more than one pension.

Most people are currently not saving enough for their later years.

Anyone can save in a pension at any age, including children and those not in paid employment.

You cannot normally take benefits from a personal pension until age 55 years.

Up to 25% of your pension can be taken as a tax-free lump sum.

The amount accumulated in a pension has traditionally been used to purchase an income for life called an annuity. Due to low annuity rates, retirees are increasingly turning to income drawdown. The radical changes in 2015 introduced more freedom & flexibility (see later).

Pension income (including state pension) is taxable.

A new flat rate state pension of £155 per week was introduced for newly retired pensioners from April 2016 but not everyone will get this amount.

The state pension age will rise for both men and women to 66 from 2020

3. Types of Pension

There are many different ways in which to save for retirement. There are schemes for public sector workers like police officers, nurses and local government employees; other pension schemes are offered as part of an employment package - frequently in larger companies. There are personal pensions, stakeholder pensions and self-invested personal pensions known as SIPPs.

Lets take a more detailed look at each of these different types of pension.

Public Sector Pension

Around 6 million public sector workers enjoy the benefits of a relatively generous occupational pension package as part of their terms of employment. The costs to the taxpayer of these pensions has been gradually increasing in recent years and there has been a lengthy process of negotiations between trades unions and government to try to implement a more sustainable public sector pensions strategy following a review by Labour peer Lord Hutton. The new plans include proposals for a higher contribution from employees, retiring later and moving from 'final salary' to 'career average' schemes.

Teachers, NHS workers, police, firefighters, the armed forces and many other public sector workers have defined benefit (or final salary) schemes. The pension they receive will depend on length of service, pensionable earnings and the schemes accrual rate which is a proportion of salary for each year of service - typically

1/80th. Therefore someone with 40 years continuous service would receive 40/80ths or half their final salary.

Pension freedom applies to defined contribution schemes and therefore most employees in the public sector would not be eligible unless they can transfer out the value of their pension to a DC scheme.

Private Sector Pension

There are around 23 million workers employed in the private sector but until the introduction of auto enrolment, less than 20% contributed to a scheme. This is in stark contrast to the public sector where over 90% of employees are members of a scheme.

Increasingly over the past 25 years, workplace **defined benefit** scheme pensions have gradually been replaced by **defined contribution** plans. Under defined benefit schemes, which were traditionally final salary plans, you built up a retirement income through a work pension plan that guaranteed you a set income for life similar to the public sector. The pension received on retirement was determined by length of service and level of pay. The employee would therefore have a good idea what pension to expect.

Under defined contribution schemes, individuals and employers typically pay into a personal pension plan provided through work and an investment pot is built up and then used to purchase an annuity, which gives an income for life. Effectively the risk has shifted from the employer to the individual worker. Employees cannot be sure what pension they will get at the end of their working lives as it will depend on several variable such as market returns, plan charges and contributions.

Workplace Pensions - Auto Enrolment

Since 2012 all employees over the age of 22 and earning over £10,000 p.a. have been automatically enrolled in their firms workplace pension. When fully rolled out by 2019, the plan is for a minimum total contribution of 8% of wages - the employee to pay in 4% of salary, the employer 3% and the taxman 1%.

The government were concerned that not enough workers were saving for retirement and introduced this new obligation on employers to try and ensure that everyone in work is enrolled in a pension scheme. By 2020 it is estimated there will be 10 million employees contributing to a workplace pension.

Of course, there have been some criticisms - the first £5,876 of pay is ignored when calculating deductions so a worker on a modest wage of £15,000 p.a. will only pay in under 5% and not 8% (from 2019) which will result in a much lower final pension pot. Part-time workers who earn less than £10,000 are not eligible as of right. I am not sure why the start age is 22 rather than 18 as contributions in the early years are important.

I understand the government are reviewing some of these issues and are planning to introduce changes but not before 2024. Personally, I think 8% is too low and particularly for those starting in their 30s and 40s.

Personal Pension

Personal Pension Plans were typically offered by banks and insurance companies. They were introduced in 1988 and replaced the retirement annuity contract. They are not so popular in recent years but may be suitable for those who are self-employed or people who don't have the benefit of a company scheme.

They may also be useful for people with savings who are not in paid employment. Charges will vary according to the type of plan you choose but typically somewhere between 1.0% and 1.8% on average. Some companies will only make plans available to those customers who have received professional advice from a financial adviser in which case the costs of such advice should also be allowed for. The minimum monthly contributions will normally be around £50 and there will be a wide range of funds on offer with most pension plan providers.

Stakeholder Pension

These are a type of personal pension and were introduced by the government in 2001 as a cheaper and more flexible alternative to the traditional personal pensions for people who did not have the benefit of a company/occupational pension. They are designed to be lower cost with fees limited to a maximum of 1.5% p.a. in the early years and reducing to 1% in later years. They are designed to be easy to understand and flexible so people should not be penalised for stopping monthly contributions or retiring early.

Historically, the choice of funds available was limited to the insurer offering the pension plan however some now offer funds from fund management groups such as Invesco Perpetual, Jupiter etc.

Stakeholder pensions are offered by most of the large insurance companies such as Aviva, Standard Life, Prudential, Legal & General etc. Plans start from as little as £25 per month.

Self Invested Personal Pension - SIPP

Sipps are also a type of personal pension and have been around since 1989. They have become more popular in recent years as more people have become comfortable taking more responsibility for their own investment decisions. This has created a larger market for sipp providers and costs have fallen which means an execution only sipp can be a very low cost option for anyone wishing to manage their own pension should they so desire.

With company schemes, the employee does not have much choice as to where and how the pension money is invested. Likewise, with personal pensions and stakeholder, the individual is often limited to the range of funds made available by the provider.

With a sipp there are no such limitations and you can choose from thousands of investment options including OEICS (unit trusts), investment trusts, exchange traded funds (ETFs), low cost trackers, bonds, commodities, gilts and corporate bonds or individual shares e.g. Vodafone, HSBC or Unilever.

Because you take responsibility for the management of your investments, an execution only SIPP is effectively a DIY pension scheme.

For those investors who are familiar with running a stocks and shares ISA via an online broker, they should have no problem implementing and managing a sipp portfolio. Indeed many people, myself included, operate both sipp and isa portfolios side by side. (I will deal with the ISA/SIPP debate in a later chapter).

For further general information I recommend The Pensions Advisory Service http://www.pensionsadvisoryservice.org.

4. State Pension

The first state pensions were introduced in 1909 under the Liberal government led by Lloyd George. They were a means tested weekly sum of up to 5 shillings per week (25p) payable from the age of 70. This would be the equivalent of around £20 today.

The modern state pension was introduced just after WW2 in 1948 and amounted to a sum of £1.30 per week for a single person and £2.10 for a married couple. Men received the pension from age 65 and women at age 60. At the time they were introduced, the average life expectancy for men was 65 years and 69 for women. Some 70 years later and the average life expectancy has risen to 81 and 84 respectively.

The Old State Pension

Entitlement to the state pension is built up over the working life through payment of national insurance contributions. Originally, the rules were that men needed 44 years of contributions and women 39 years. In 2010, this was reduced to 30 years for both men and women. Credits were usually given for periods of unemployment and for parents (usually women) taking time away from work to bring up children or time spent as a carer.

From April 2018 the old basic state pension increased to £126 per week. Pensioners with limited or no savings may also be entitled to pension credit which is designed to guarantee a minimum pension income of currently £163 for a single person and £248.80 for a couple.

Although pension credit is means tested, the basic state pension is not.

People who reached state pension age before April 2016 will continue under the old system which has two basic elements, the basic pension and secondly, for many but not all, additional pension such as State Earnings Related Pension Scheme - SERPS which was later replaced by State Second Pension - S2P. Both provided workers earning above certain limits with additional entitlements to supplement the basic pension. However the schemes were very complex and almost impossible for the average worker to understand.

However, many workers in final salary pension schemes and also public sector employees did not qualify for these additional state pension. They paid lower NICs and would rely on a pension from their employer's scheme plus the basic state pension. These people were 'contracted out' of the state scheme.

New Flat Rate State Pension

We are all living a lot longer as a result of advances in health care and better living standards. The Office for National Statistics estimates that 50% of all babies born in 2017 will reach the age of 100.

The national cost of paying state pensions has been increasing to a point where it would soon become unaffordable and unsustainable unless some radical changes were made.

When you compare how working patterns have changed since the 1950s and 60s, it's not surprising we need to save a lot more for our retirement. It used to be the case that many people started work at the age of 14 or 15 yrs and worked for up to 45 or even 50 years and then were retired for an average of 10 years. Nowadays, it seems that we expect to work for 35 years and be retired for 35 as well. The sums simply don't add up

As many people will know, the state pension age for women has been gradually rising from 60 to 65 years. From 2020 the age at which both men and women receive their state pensions will be increased and equalised at 66 yrs. It is proposed that the state pension age will rise to 67 years from 2028 and than rise again to 68 from 2037.

In April 2016, the government introduced its non means tested flat rate state pension. The starting amount was £155 per week and will rise in line with inflation, average wages or a minimum of 2.5% each year. The rate increased to £164.35 per week (£8,546 p.a.) from April 2018.

Those people who reached state pension age before April 2016 will continue under the old system.

For millions of people, the state pension will be their main source of income in retirement. No adjustment is made for variation in life expectancy - the longer you live, the more you receive.

As with the 'old' pensions, the triple lock provisions will ensure that the new pensions are increased each year to keep pace with inflation, however this provision is under review and may well change after 2022.

The new pensions are designed to be less complex and fairer - whether this happens in practice is less certain!

The period of qualifying years by way of NI contributions (or credits) has increased from 30 to 35 years. You will need a minimum of 10 years NICs before you qualify for the new pension.

The state second pension (S2P) has been removed and therefore, after 2016 there will be no more contracting out. Those workers who have previously been contracted out therefore pay higher NI contributions (as will their employers).

There are proposals to link the pension age to life expectancy age and this will be reviewed by Parliament every 5 years.

The removal of the means tested uplift by way of the pension savings credit is designed to encourage more people to save for the future.

The increase to £164 per week, is designed to provide a basic income for everyone with a full 35 yr NIC record however, not everyone will receive this flat rate amount.

It will be reduced for those workers who do not have the full 35 yr NIC record. Therefore someone with only 25 yrs NI contributions would get 25/35ths or £117 per week. For each missing year, the amount would therefore be reduced by £4.68.

Secondly, it will be reduced for those who have been contracted out. This is because the DWP is factoring in what they might have built up in a private pension due to lower or diverted NI contributions during the time they were contracted out. They refer to this as the 'COPE' amount (contracted out pension equivalent). Many workers would not have been aware of whether they were contracted out or not and national insurance contributions would be deducted automatically from pay packets without the employee realising it was a lower rate.

Millions of workers in both public and private sector will have been contracted out as they will have been members of a defined benefit pension scheme and paying a lower level of NI. It is estimated that less than half of newly retired pensioners from April 2016 receive the full flat rate payment.

Some pensioners will have built up entitlements under SERPS and S2P which would provide much more than the basic state pension. Many will therefore get more than the flat rate £164 per week.

The DWP will undertake two calculations, one under the old system and one under the new system and the claimant will receive the higher of these calculations. Therefore, under the new state pension arrangements, no one will get less than the amount that they would have received under the old rules based on their own NI record, as long as they meet the minimum qualifying period of 10 years of NI contributions or credits.

Finally, although you will need a minimum 35 yrs NICs to qualify for the full pension, workers will get no additional pension when they pay in for more years.

It will take many years for these anomalies to drop out of the system. It is estimated that by 2030 the majority of pensioners will be entitled to the full flat rate pension.

To get a statement of how much State Pension you could get, you can contact the **Future Pension Centre** www.gov.uk/check-state-pension

National Insurance Credits

National Insurance credits are a way of maintaining your NI record when you are not making National Insurance contributions. They help to build up 'qualifying years', which count towards your entitlement for basic state pension.

It will therefore be important to build a full 35 yr NI record if you are to qualify for the maximum state pension. Those in regular employment will normally have NI deducted from their pay automatically. The self employed will normally be liable for Class 2 and Class 4 contributions depending on the level of profits for the year.

Those who are unable to work due to illness or who have responsibilities as a carer or who are bringing up young children can get NI credits.

For example, parents who receive Child Benefit and are caring for a child under the age of 12 receive National Insurance credits automatically.

As noted earlier, each 'missing' year will result in a reduction of $1/35^{th}$ of your state pension currently worth £4.68 per week or a loss of £243 each year - more as the state pension increases year on year.

For further details:-

https://www.gov.uk/national-insurance-credits/eligibility

Pension Delay

You can put off claiming your basic state pension. This can be especially useful if you're still working, as it means you'll get larger pension payments later.

For each year you postpone taking your state pension, you get the full pension plus 5.8% extra. It is estimated that if you delay for one year (lose £8,500) you will need to live a further 18 years before you start to gain on the deal. The longer you live, the more benefit you get - but it's obviously a gamble.

Proposed Changes to State Pensions

Although the universal state pension is likely to be around in its present form for some years to come, many economists and finance commentators are starting to suggest the state pension may not be affordable for everyone in the longer term.

The state pension is dependent on 'pay-as-you-go' funding which means we do not build up our personal 'pot' of pension but a system whereby today's workers pay for today's pensioners. As time goes by and because we are living longer, there will be fewer workers paying for more and more pensioners. This raises an issue of fairness for younger people.

An independent review chaired by former CBI boss John Cridland is suggesting a number of changes to make pensions more sustainable in the longer term. They include:

* raising the state pension age to 68 from 2037

* scrapping the triple lock and linking rises to just earnings

* provisions to delay taking pensions in return for an up-front lump sum payment

In a submission to a review looking at state pensions, the Association of Consulting Actuaries said:

"On the assumption that, in aggregate, longevity continues to improve, whilst significant differences in life expectancy continue to exist between different sectors of society, we believe that the retention of a universal but rising State Pension Age will become increasingly difficult."

The government finances are increasingly under pressure from an increase in the population, the fact we are all living longer and the associated increases to fund our social services and NHS. Spending on pensions has doubled over the past 10 years and is currently running at over £100bn every year.

The government has relied on borrowing to bridge the gap between the money it receives in taxes etc. and the ever increasing demands placed upon the public purse. Despite implementing cutbacks and austerity measures since 2010, the national debt has continued to rise and rise (£1.8 trillion Nov 2017).

At some point down the line, there may come a point when pensions could be subject to means testing and perhaps only paid in full to those with no other provision.

Therefore, although the state pension will continue for some time, younger people just starting out in the world of work would be well advised to think seriously about saving in a works and/or private pension or sipp and take more responsibility for their future financial security.

Of course, many people would like a little more than 'basic' state pension in their retirement years. They may also like the option of retiring a little earlier than state pension age which is likely to rise to 70 for younger people.

To do either or both will require a serious commitment to saving combined with a long term plan.

5. Personal Pension

There are a lot of misconceptions and mystery surrounding this subject for the average person. This really does not need to be the case and one of the main reasons for writing this guide is to help ordinary men and women better **understand the basics of pensions** and, hopefully, to encourage them to take more responsibility for their future financial security.

So, what is a pension?

In its stripped back, simplest form a pension is a tax efficient way of saving money over a long period of time - 20, 30 or even 40 years. When the money goes in, it is locked away - you can't get at it, your employer can't get it (they sometimes contribute), your creditors can't get it. When you stop working, the money is returned to you with interest and you will have a number of options.

The earlier you start, the more chance the pension 'pot' has to grow - its called the magic of compound returns. Additionally, the government is very keen to encourage everyone to contribute towards a pension so, for every £80 you put in, the taxman will throw in a further £20. Put it another way…for every £4 you pay in, you get a further £1 for free or if you are a higher rate tax payer, for every £3 you pay in, you get a further £2 for free.

If you save hard and invest it wisely and do not incur too much in the way of charges, there's a very good chance you will build a very useful pension pot by the time you come to retire. Indeed, you may do so well, you are able to retire early.

How much to pay in?

It depends on the level of income needed in retirement and the time horizon between starting a pension and retirement age - the longer the better!

Some people have no idea what percentage of savings will be required to provide the level of income needed to retire on.

As a rough rule of thumb, use half your age when you start the pension and this is the percentage to pay in. So, starting at age 24yrs, you pay in 12% of your gross income. Someone starting aged 40 yrs would pay 20% of income etc.

If your employer is contributing, include their share as part of the total percentage.

When you get a pay increase, remember to increase the pension contributions.

Most people under estimate the size of pension pot required to produce the income they would ideally like when they retire.

A report in May 2018 by former pensions minister Steve Webb for Royal London suggested that the average person needs to save £260,000 over their lifetime to enjoy a basic income in retirement and a staggering £445,000 if they do not get on the property ladder. They expect that around a third of retirees will be renting and will need to find an additional £6,554 in rent to private landlords.

The introduction of the flat rate pension in 2016 should make it easier to plan ahead as you should have a clearer picture of what state pension to expect - currently £8,500, however the report calculated that the average person will need an additional £9,000 on top of the basic state pension to enjoy a reasonable standard of living.

So what amount of pension pot should I aim for ?

Lets assume you will get the full basic state pension of £164 per week (say £8,500 p.a.). To generate this sort of income at today's annuity rates would require a pot of around £200,000. Therefore to get a pension income around the average wage level of around £400 per week - £20,000 p.a. - you would require a pension pot to generate an extra £11,500 per year on top of the state pension.

To generate this additional £11,500 p.a. means you would require a total pension pot of around £275,000. This figure is around £200,000 more than the current average. Remember, all pension income is taxable - state and private - so you may need to allow for a deduction of tax from some of this income.

Hopefully, the above will give a rough estimation of the sums involved and individuals can get some idea of the calculations to be made to produce the desired level of income.

Of course, you can easily look up an online pension calculator and play around with various figures. One of the better ones I've found is at the Hargreaves Lansdown website.

Also worth a look - http://www.candidmoney.com/calculators/retirement-age-calculator

Will it matter if I delay for a few years?

Yes! The earlier you start, the better your chances of maximising your pension pot. Having said that, its never too late to start.

Consider the following:

To explore the power of compound returns lets take Alex and Sue.

From the age of 25, Sue invests £2,000 per year in her personal pension for 10 years until she is 35 - a total contribution of £20,000. At 35 she stops working to start a family and never puts any further contributions into the pension.

Sue leaves her pension pot untouched to grow until she retires at the age of 65. Her fund earns an average annual return of 8% and when she looks at her statement of account 30 years later, she is pleased to see the pot has grown to **£346,161**.

Alex, meanwhile, spends all his earnings between the ages of 25 to 35 having a good time. Its only at the ripe old age of 35 that he thinks he had better do something about his pension. He starts to put away £2,000 per year in his SIPP . He manages to keep this going for the next 30 years - a total contribution of £60,000 - until he also retires at the age of 65.

Alex's pension also earns an average annual return of 8%. He ends up with a total of only **£244,691**.

So, we can see quite clearly the big difference between starting early and delaying by 10 years. Alex contributed 3x more than Sue but ended up with over £100K less.

There are several factors which will combine to determine the size of our final pension pot - our level of earnings, how early we start saving, how late we retire, the charges on our pension fund and the rate of return generated by the investments. We may not have much control over some of these elements but one factor we can determine is when we start to save - clearly, the sooner the better.

Research in the USA revealed that starting a pension at 25 yrs rather than 45 yrs will reduce the required savings percentage by two thirds. In his book 'The Investor's Manifesto' William Bernstein described how for each pound you do not save at age 25 means you will need to save £2 at age 35, £4 at 45 and £8 starting at age 55.

Tax Relief for High Earners

Tax relief is available on pension contributions. For most earners on average wages, this will be the standard 20%. Therefore, for every £100 contribution from you, HMRC will contribute £25 which is 20% of the gross combined amount.

Higher rate tax payers get 40% tax relief on their contributions so effectively the gross combined amount of £125 would mean they only contribute £75 and HMRC £50. Top rate tax payers would pay only £68.75.

Furthermore, pension contributions effectively expand your basic rate tax band. <u>Any pension contributions are deducted from salary before it is taxed. People would normally be liable for 40% income tax on earnings over £46,350 (2018/19). So if you earn say £50,000 you would pay £1,460 tax at 40% on the £3,650 above the threshold, however if you were to pay 8% of your earnings - £4,000 into a pension this would effectively take you out of the higher rate tax bracket.</u>

The above reflects the tax situation at the time of publication but may be subject to changes in subsequent taxation legislation.

Director of Small Limited Company

For those running a small business as a limited company, there are significant tax advantages from pension contributions. They can be treated as an allowable business expense and therefore will be offset against the company's corporation tax liability.

Directors can make personal contributions or the company can make contributions.

With a personal contribution, directors normally take a combination of salary and dividends, however the dividend part does not count as 'relevant earnings' so the amount taken as salary will be used to calculate pension tax relief limit.

With employer contributions from the company, these are made from pre-tax profits and therefore the company receives relief against corporation tax (19% for 2018/19). In addition, the company will not be liable for National Insurance on pension contributions so combined with CT, the saving would be 32.8%.

You therefore have the three options for contributions - personal, company or both. It will of course make sense for directors to discuss these options with their accountant.

What about charges?

I guess many of today's pensioners may have held some sort of private pension plan. They will have saved hard over maybe 30 or 40 years and find when the time comes to retire, the amount they are offered is much less than they imagined. One reason for this is the effect of falling gilt yields on annuity rates - by the end of 2016, gilt yields were at their lowest point for over 100 years.

A further factor, however, will be the effect of the annual management charges, underlying fund costs, dealing fees, and introductory/trail commissions paid to intermediaries which all contribute to depleting returns. In October 2014 the National Association of Pension Funds admitted that fees were too high and that consumers face an 'eye wateringly complex' system of hidden levies.

A pension fund worth almost £250,000 with no charges would be reduced to just £174,556 after 40 years, with just a 1.5% annual charge (typical for the average managed pension fund). By increasing the annual charge to 2.5%, this would reduce the value of the fund to £139,986 - a reduction of 44%!

What is not often clearly spelt out is that this annual management charge refers to the percentage of the fund that is taken each year, rather than the percentage of the money invested. So in the first year if you invested £5,000 and there was no growth, this would be just a £75 fee. But after 20 years, if there was no growth at all and you invested £5,000 a year, you would be paying £1,265 in charges, so almost a quarter of your annual contributions would be disappearing in charges.

I have done a comparison based on contributions of £250 per month over a period of 35 years - a total contribution of £105,000. Growth is assumed at 6% per year.

A low cost sipp invested via a Vanguard tracker with costs of 0.25% would be valued at £324,000. The old style pension plan which levied initial charges of 5% and annual charges of 1.5% would be valued at just £233,000. That's a staggering £91,000 more in your pension pot just for choosing the low cost option.

I think a lot of people may be surprised by such figures and the dramatic impact seemingly small differences in charges can make when compounded over a lengthy period of time.

The main point to be made is charges for the average managed pension fund have generally been too high as well as too complex and should be avoided if you want a decent return on your contributions over the long haul. I would urge everyone who has an existing personal pension to check out the charges to ensure they are aware of exactly how much is being taken from their fund.

For further reading on investment charges (and many other issues) I can recommend Pete Comley's '**Monkey With a Pin**' (free ebook download available from www.Amazon.co.uk)

Also, a useful online calculator:
http://www.candidmoney.com/calculators/investment-fund-cost-comparison-calculator

Do I need a Financial Adviser?

Increasingly, with the introduction of work-based auto enrolment pensions, many people will join their company scheme which will have been set up in consultation with pension experts or more likely, the NEST scheme.

For people who do not have this option e.g. self employed, it will be a matter of personal choice. Some will have quite complex financial arrangements and will probably need expert guidance, others may just feel more reassured to receive guidance from a pensions specialist.

In the past there have been many instances of mis-selling and the financial services industry has struggled to retain the confidence of the general public at times. Much of this poor practice was due to the fact that pensions carried high commission levels and it was therefore very tempting for salesmen, remunerated largely via commission payments, to favour products that, shall we say, were not always in the customers best interest.

With the introduction of the Retail Distribution Review (RDR) in 2014, sales commission has been abolished and the charging structure is now more transparent. Hopefully, the consumer will now receive a much better service from financial advisers. To find an adviser in your area - www.unbiased.co.uk

The average pension saver will have fairly modest monthly savings to invest. In the past, the cost of financial advice was hidden as most advisers would be paid from the commission rolled up within the fund charges. The introduction of the Retail Distribution Review has changed this arrangement and the costs of advice is now paid upfront and should be clearly agreed at the outset. This will result in fewer, but better qualified advisers who will probably be targeting those clients who can more easily afford the up-front fees.

These initial advice fees typically range from £750 to £2,000 plus vat depending on the degree of complexity and the investment amounts involved. In addition, there may well be some ongoing annual review which will involve further fees - typically £500 plus vat. Those with more modest pension requirements may well find they either cannot afford these fees or just see them as a deterrent to seeking professional advice. These people will be increasingly left to fend for themselves and this could possibly mean either DIY or possibly turning to the services of an online wealth manager or robo advisor.

There is therefore the potential to save a great deal of money by taking a little time to understand the basics and considering the option of pursuing a simple diy approach.

For those prepared to read around the subject and who do not have complicated finances and who feel comfortable in taking more responsibility for their financial affairs, it is possible to arrange a pension on a DIY basis and this book is designed to assist those who want to go down that route.

Possibly a Robo Advisor?

Robo Advisors or online wealth managers as they prefer to be called are fairly new to the UK but have been around in the USA for some time. The most well-known would be the likes of Vanguard, Schwab, Wealthfront and Betterment who manage around $70 billion of clients pension investments between them.

They aim to provide a solution to those who cannot afford a traditional face-to-face advisor and those who do not have the confidence to go it alone.

Basically, the client will sign up with one of the growing number of firms providing this service - more well-known ones are Nutmeg and Moneyfarm for example. They then complete an online risk assessment to determine and gather other information such as time horizon, age and experience which they then use sophisticated algorithms to build a suggested low cost portfolio of funds using mainly ETFs.

Obviously the attraction for the novice or less confident investor is the provision of a service which des not involve large up-front charges combined with the fact that you do not need to research and select your own investments which makes it very easy to make a start with pension saving. The fees charged are generally between 0.75% and 1.0% of the sum(s) invested and this is likely to be considerably less than you would pay for a professional advisor which is typically 2% or 3%.

For those who wish to go it alone but require a second opinion on asset allocation, it may be worthwhile going through the preliminary questions to see what mix of equities/bonds are suggested by one or more of these firms.

For those who wish to investigate in a little more detail, I have listed a few of the more popular firms at the end of the book.

6. Planning for Retirement

As life expectancy rises, many people can expect to work for up to 45 years followed by up to 35 years of retirement. They often don't fully appreciate how much they need to save and over what time period to generate enough of a pension pot to provide a comfortable retirement. As the state pension age - currently 65 - rises, many people will find they will need to keep working a lot longer than they anticipated.

The 45 years of work is when the pension pot will be gradually accumulated. The pot will grow in several ways, firstly via the monthly/annual contributions, secondly via the 25% tax credits courtesy of HMRC and finally via growth of the existing fund as any dividends and/or interest are continually reinvested and investments increase their capital value.

According to industry statistics, the average personal pension pot is currently only around £65,000, so someone retiring today is likely to be offered an annuity of less than £3,000 per year. Factor in the current basic state pension of £6,400 (old) or £8,500 (new) and its not hard to see why many pensioners will be struggling. In fact, around 40% of today's pensioners are in receipt of means tested pension credit.

To try to avoid ending up in a similar situation it is important for younger people to start saving sooner rather than later and to avoid high fund charges. You really do not want to get to your 60s and be pinning your hopes on winning the national lottery for a comfortable retirement.

As we have seen, some people are offered some sort of pension package as part of their employment. A common scheme is where you pay a certain percentage of your wage into the company pension which is matched by the employer. I cannot think of a good reason why any employee would not wish to join a company scheme, however according to a report from the Office for National Statistics (2014), the number of people saving into a workplace pension had fallen below 50%. The introduction of the workplace auto-enrolment pension should gradually start to reverse this percentage.

However, if a company pension scheme is not available, or if you are self-employed as a sole trader or in a partnership, you will need to set up a personal/stakeholder pension or a self-invested pension called a sipp. The SIPP has become more popular over recent years as more people realise they can take control of their own investment decisions.

Before we go further, it will be useful to have a look at some of the aspects relating to the big picture which will be a blueprint of basically where you want to get to with your retirement plans, when you want to arrive and how you will develop your strategy.

The Outline Plan

An essential first step is to develop a broad outline of a plan setting out what you want to achieve and how you will go about achieving your goals. Things to include might be :

- a target retirement age, when would you like to retire? 45, 55, 65

- what amount of yearly income would you need? (see below)

- what is your target figure? £250,000, £600,000

- what about asset allocation - what level of equities?

- what level of annual return will your fund deliver? 5%, 7% ?
(Over the longer periods, equities tend to produce a higher return than bonds and fixed interest).

- active or passive investing strategy ?

- what level of contributions can you afford? £200 per month, £500 per month

- what other assets can you reasonably factor in? Other savings, property, inheritance.

These are some of the initial questions you will need to address to formulate your overall plan and strategy.

If you are unsure about your plans, try using one of the online retirement planners. One example is on the Pensions Advisory Service website -

www.pensionsadvisoryservice.org.uk/my-pension/online-planners

As you gain more knowledge and experience of managing your pension, you will probably wish to review your plan - are the targets still realistic and achievable? Is it possible to increase contributions? Am I getting the returns I require etc. etc?

Work Out Your Target Figure

There are two basic questions to be addressed - what level of income do I need when retired and secondly, what level of savings will be needed to provide that income?

So, although this is not a precise science and each individuals circumstances and preferences will vary, here is the outline of a few basic steps I have used for my own planning process in working out a figure.

1. Set a target date for your ideal retirement - it may need to change as the calculations unfold.

2. If you know what income you need fine, otherwise take your current annual net income and deduct any mortgage expense as this will likely be repaid. Then deduct 20% as this is the average work-related expense you will not have to spend when retired. So, if your mortgage is £5,000 p.a. your take home pay is £30,000 this target figure would be £20,000 (£25K less 20%).

3. If you have a works and/or personal pension or SIPP, get a projection of the annual amount(s) to be paid and deduct from the above figure.

4. Multiply the remaining sum by 25 to provide you with a ballpark capital sum needed to generate the remaining income.

Therefore if the replacement income figure after deducting works pensions was £12,000, the lump sum needed to generate this annual income would be £300,000 (£12K x 25). This is based on a reasonably sustainable return of 4% p.a. from the investments.

If you intend to bridge the gap between early retirement and state pension, for example 10 yrs from age 57 to 67, it may be an option to use a lower multiplier figure of say x 18 (rather than x 25) which would obviously reduce the lump sum target figure - in the above example from £300K to £216K. The income taken from the lower sum would be nearer 6% p.a. which would be less sustainable long term but certainly a feasible option over 10 yrs.

5. Once you have settled on a final figure and you know the number of years from now to your retirement date, work out what level of savings from your current income would be needed to reach this figure.

There are many online calculators available - I use Candid Money http://www.candidmoney.com/calculators/ To generate £300,000 in the above example would take just over 20 yrs saving at 20% of salary assuming 6% average return.

If you are saving via a pension or the new lifetime ISA remember to factor in the HMRC tax credits to your contributions when using these calculators.

6. If your retirement date is close to your state pension age of 66 or 67, remember to factor this additional income ~£8,000 p.a. into the calculations. In the above example, the £12,000

therefore reduces to just £4,000 and the lump sum required comes down from £300K to £100K.

A Look At Early Planned Retirement

Some people are really happy and content in their work and would not consider giving it up.

However, most of us will at some point in our lives have dreamt of an early retirement. Giving up the early morning commute and the 9 to 5 drudge and freeing up time to pursue the things we love doing - travelling, writing, spending more time with family, hobbies…the list is endless.

Sadly, for most, this remains a dream and more and more workers expect to continue working well past 60 and even into their 70s.

The stepping stones to an early retirement consist of three elements :

1. Make a start - the sooner in life the better, and

2. Have a good plan and stick to it, finally,

3. Spend much less than you earn.

Many people believe they are doing well if they manage to save 10% of their income every month…and they are, its better than not saving. However, if you can get into the habit of saving 25% of your income in your 20s and invest wisely, you will be in a position to retire 10 years earlier.... save 50% and you could retire in your 40s.

There are currently many thousands of young people in the UK who have embraced the concept of FIRE - financial independence, retire early. They realise that much of what the average person spends is based upon wasteful consumerism where wall to wall advertising encourages everyone to spend more and more of their income on stuff they don't really need.

Buoyed by mass advertising, the marketing strategy of planned obsolescence - which entails industry manufacturing goods deliberately designed to break or become out of date quickly - is used to hook us into the mass consumer frenzy which teaches us that in order to have value and happiness, we must spend, spend, spend. Easy credit also helps, of course.

Reports suggest we consume twice as many material goods as our parents generation. Some people are asking the question "Why do we carry on buying more and more stuff than we actually need?" To successfully answer this question could free up lives and resources for more meaningful and important pursuits.

Rejecting this treadmill of spending can free people to work out what they really value and spend on the things they genuinely need. As a result they find they can save up to 50% of their net income without much compromise to their happiness or standard of living.

Having worked your way through these steps and maybe played around with a number of different calculations, it is time to make a decision.

Is it worth cutting back on all but essentials and increasing the savings rate to 40% or 50% to bring forward the retirement date by maybe 20 yrs like my fellow blogger and author Robert Tracey has recently achieved?
http://www.retirementinvestingtoday.com/

If you are the type of person who could happily live on 50% of your income, maybe you could manage on salary minus 40% or 50%. In the example above for the person earning £30,000, the multiplier would be based on £15,000 - so 25x gives a target of £375,000. (There would be no deduction for the works pension as this would not usually be available until age 60 yrs).

Saving £1,250 p.m. in a Stocks & Shares ISA with an average return of 6% per year and allowing 0.5% for platform/fund costs would take approximately 16 years to achieve the above target amount.

The target figure could be reached much sooner using a SIPP due to the effect of tax credits added to the contributions. However, pensions could not be accessed until the person was 57 yrs so this would generally not be a good option for those starting in their 20s or 30s.

I will return to a sustainable withdrawal rate later in the book, however the target amount should be sufficient to generate an annual income of £15,000 for the rest of your life.

Finally, for those who may be pursuing early retirement, be aware that to qualify for a full state pension, you will need 35 years of national insurance contributions (or credits). Therefore, if you were to retire after working for say 25 years, you would need to consider paying voluntary Class 3 contributions for 10 years to cover the gap in your NI record. The current rate for 2017/18 is £741 p.a.

Each years contribution will add 1/35th to your state pension in the future, currently worth around £236 which means the annual outlay to purchase the contributions would be recouped after 4 years.

So, once you have all the information, settled on your ideal retirement date and worked through the various calculations, you can make an informed choice. Without doing the above, you are not really in control of two important elements - how early you can retire and how much you will receive.

Pay into Pension or Pay Off Mortgage

Clearing the mortgage and building a retirement lump sum are possibly two of the most common financial goals.

A mortgage is a debt and common sense dictates that there is little point in saving until the debts are cleared. I would certainly agree with this when it comes to credit card debt and personal loans as the interest is usually relatively high.

However, when it comes to saving for retirement, it may not be a smart decision to wait 25 yrs for your mortgage to be paid off before starting to save for retirement.

The two factor which possibly tip the balance in favour of the pension are inflation and tax relief.

The mortgage is usually repaid by a fixed sum each month representing capital and interest. Over time, these payments will fall in value due to inflation so after say 10 years, they represent a smaller percentage of your wages which will have been gradually increasing.

Secondly, each £1,000 invested in a pension will be boosted to £1,250 courtesy of HMRC and £1,400 for higher rate tax payers. The effect of the added tax relief combined with the investment growth of maybe 6% p.a. over the length of an average mortgage will almost certainly give a better outcome compared to repaying a mortgage with an interest rate of 6%.

Of course there are lots of variables and unknown factors over such a lengthy period. Mortgage interest rates have been low for the past few years but they could well increase. Likewise, although the returns on investments have averaged 6% or 7% over the past 20 years, they could be lower over the next 20 years.

The choice therefore is not clear cut and some people like the immediate benefit of seeing their mortgage debt reducing year-on-year as the value of their property increases. Furthermore, the increased equity in the property may provide opportunities for a better re-mortgage opportunity down the line.

7. Building the DIY Pension Pot

Once the plans are in place you can start to put them into practice. As mentioned earlier, the self invested personal pension or SIPP has become very popular over the past decade as there are many low cost providers and more people have access to the technology to make it relatively simple to operate this type of pension.

I have held a sipp for many years since I wanted to consolidate several pension plans with different insurance companies and take more control of my investments. In 2012, I started to take benefits from my sipp by way of income drawdown and in 2015 I converted to flexi-drawdown under the new pension freedom rules which essentially mean I can now take as much or as little as I require from my pension.

For me, the SIPP is the ideal vehicle to build a diy pension.

A SIPP can be the Ideal Option

For maximum investment options combined with minimal cost, the execution only SIPP is possibly the best option for someone wishing to take control of personal pension planning. (By the way, execution only means the sipp provider offers no advice as to how your contributions are invested).

It provides you with the flexibility and freedom to decide exactly how, where and in what proportions your pension contributions are to be invested. This is in contrast to the personal or stakeholder pension administered by the large insurance companies and where you have a more limited range of options to select from.

Last year the number of sipps in operation increased over 50% and the figure is expected to exceed 2 million by 2020.

The demand for execution only sipps is likely to continue growing as savvy investors become more aware of pension advice costs following the implementation of the Retail Distribution Review (RDR). These people are also becoming more confident in managing their financial affairs via the internet and mobile trading apps.

Selecting a Provider

Having prepared a plan, the next step is to select a suitable low cost sipp provider. My own choice has been AJ Bell's YouInvest as they could offer the package I required for a lump sum SIPP using mainly investment trusts for which no platform charges were levied (this changed in 2016) - no transfer-in fees (as I intended to consolidate a number of personal pensions), a wide range of investment options and competitive fees on both execution of trades and, in retirement, for the benefits stage like income/flexi drawdown.

It is important to consider the charges relating to taking benefits in retirement as it can be costly to transfer your pension to another provider at a later date. Other providers may be equally as good. Some common choices could be Halifax Sharedealing, iWeb, Hargreaves Lansdown Vantage Sipp, Charles Stanley Direct, Alliance Trust and BestInvest.

Some providers may be better for a traditional funds-based investment approach including index funds, others will be competitive for investing in shares and investment trusts or exchange traded funds.

Low cost index funds are becoming more popular with small investors. The ongoing charges for some are less than 0.10% which is incredibly good value but this can be negated by holding them in a sipp with percentage charges which apply up to say £250K. A similar product may be available as an ETF with a slightly higher ongoing charge but because the platform costs are capped, the combined costs will work out less than holding the lower cost index fund.

An extra 0.20% in broker platform charges may not seem much but on an typical sipp portfolio of around £50,000 it will be an extra £100 every year. On a larger portfolio of £200K the extra charges would be £400 every year.

If you are intending to use mainly low cost trackers, it will obviously be essential to make sure the particular ones you require are offered by your selected provider and that any additional platform fees are economical for the size of holding you have.

Some providers do not make a dealing charge for regular purchase of funds so this option is obviously attractive for those making regular monthly contributions to their pension. It's a good idea to try to automate the process as much as possible.

SIPP providers broadly fall into two groups:

those that charge a **percentage fee** which are obviously good if you have smaller amounts invested - possibly the norm for most investors in the early years;

and those that charge a **flat fee** which is possibly the better choice for larger sums.

Make a careful list of your particular requirements then visit the websites of all potential sipp providers to establish which provider will best tick the most boxes for you.

To assist with this process, you may want to compare platforms and their charges on the following websites. Just be aware that it is a possibility that not all platforms choose to participate so you may need to check these separately. Use this as a start but it should not be the end of selection process.

www.comparefundplatforms.com
www.monevator.com

Another advantage of the sipp, is that it can be used to consolidate any number of assorted personal pensions built up in the past and which may be with different providers and possibly with relatively higher costs involved. It can be very useful to see the total value of all your pensions when they are brought together in one place.

If consolidation is something you are considering, it will be worth checking whether there are any transfer-in costs when selecting your sipp.

(**NB** Some pension plans, particularly older plans e.g. retirement annuity contracts, may have valuable guarantees attached so you would be advised to check with your provider as these guarantees can be lost when transferred out.)

Asset Allocation & Attitude to Risk

A significant part of the planning process will involve asset allocation. By this we mean building a diverse portfolio - what percentage to place in equities, how much in bonds, UK or global focus, should I have some emerging markets exposure or property, what about smaller companies?

As we have seen, one big factor affecting long term returns will be costs - this will include platform fees and ongoing annual charges of selected investments, so the lower the better. However, another significant factor is not so much working out which share or low cost tracker to buy, but what proportion of your steadily growing wealth should be invested in each category or asset class.

I believe diversification by asset class, geography and strategy is a one of the best forms of risk management.

As an example, if you are young and/or adventurous, you may decide to allocate a larger percentage of your investments in equities. If so, what proportion will be UK and what proportion will be global or other geographic areas? Will there be some proportion allocated to medium cap and smaller companies? Will you stick with equities in developed economies like Europe and USA or will you diversify into faster growing developing economies like South America and China? The important thing is to consider all the options and then make an informed choice and have an understanding of what you want to achieve.

There are many different ways to invest. UK shares (equities), overseas shares e.g. USA or China, government bonds (gilts), corporate bonds, commercial property, commodities like gold or oil, and cash are just a few. Some assets are relatively safe and stable e.g. gilts and cash deposits, other assets are more volatile and risky such as individual shares or emerging markets funds but they may offer the prospects of better returns over the longer term.

Many people will naturally be wary of things they don't understand, others will be determined not to lose the money they have saved hard to accumulate. Others will be adventurous and invest in South American AIM listed mining shares and oil explorers - obviously a high risk, high reward strategy.

Somewhere in between these two positions is a point where many will wish to find some balance with which they feel comfortable. There is a tendency for younger people to be more adventurous as they have more time to make amends if things don't quite go according to plan. Older people will tend to be more conservative with more focus on capital preservation.

Know Yourself

When first starting out on the investing journey, I believe one of the least understood aspects is probably the need for every investor to understand their unique emotional make up and ability to withstand the volatility of the markets and then to match this to the most appropriate allocation of assets taking into account time horizon.

Successful investing via a pension is all about the long term so it is vitally important to 'stay in the game' for many years. It is therefore crucially important at the start of the process to find an investment process and strategy that meshes well with your personality and temperament. This is probably an area I did not fully consider at the start of my own sipp journey so I hope would-be diy pension investors can avoid the same mistake!

This is a long term project so it is essential to select a strategy that will give you the best chance of staying in the game - particularly when the markets are volatile. Finding the correct balance between equities and bonds (and other assets) and matching this with your psychological makeup will be the **key to a successful outcome**.

Charlie Ellis 'Winning the Loser's Game'
"The hardest work in investing is not intellectual, its emotional. Being rational in an emotional environment is not easy. The hardest work is not figuring out the best investment policy; its sustaining a long term focus at market highs or market lows and remaining committed to a sound investment policy. Its hard especially when Mr Market always tries to trick you into making changes".

Most people understand the benefits of not putting all your eggs in one basket. By diversifying your investments between different areas, you will spread the risk.

A simple allocation could be:

50% Global Equities,
25% UK Gilts,

15% Corporate Bonds, and
10% Property

Other options could include commodities, emerging markets, physical gold or silver, smaller companies etc. etc.

As time goes by, these percentages will change as one class of asset does better than another. It is therefore important to rebalance the portfolio from time to time, say at the end of each year. It may be that global equities sector have gone up to 60% by the end of the first year, so sell off the gain of 10% in this sector which has done well and reinvest the proceeds between the other categories to restore the original allocation balance.

Over time, the fund will grow year-on-year and each year that passes will bring you closer to the eventual retirement date. It is important to re-evaluate your spread of assets periodically. Many people will think it sensible to reduce equities and increase gilts and bonds as you get nearer to retirement.

My personal preference, having converted my sipp to income drawdown in 2012, was to maintain a 60% equities/40% bonds and fixed interest balance well past retirement as I needed the extra growth provided by equities to provide a rising income during the period before state pension age. In this sense, the drawdown option can be similar to an index-linked annuity.

Because pensions are long term investments, equities are more likely to produce better returns than cash or bonds. Research carried out by Barcap Equity/Gilt Study has established that since 1900, the real returns per year (i.e. after allowing for inflation) for each category has been, cash 1.0%, bonds 1.9% and equities (shares) 5.0%.

Over shorter periods the returns can be very variable. For example over the 10 yrs to 2017 the comparative figures were, cash -1.3% (very low interest rates), bonds 4.3% and equities 2.5%.

Active or Passive?

The next decision is the style of investment approach - this will fall into two broad categories, active or passive. Active investing involves you selecting shares, actively managed funds or investment trusts which you consider will deliver a consistently good return over many years.

Passive investing involves the purchase of one or more low cost trackers i.e. funds or exchange traded funds (ETFs) which aim to track a particular index e.g. FTSE 100.

If I were starting out today, my personal choice based on low costs and ease of use would be a passive approach. Lets look at this in a little more detail.

Passive Investing

Unless stock market investing is a hobby, you probably don't have the time or inclination to undertake a great deal of research on investments. All you want is a simple approach to invest your monthly contributions which is likely to provide a better return over the long run than the majority of professional investment managers.

To achieve this you can invest in low cost index funds which track the market(s) you are interested in. These index funds will hold all the individual shares which make up the index. So instead of buying shares in all 100 companies which make up the FTSE 100, you buy a FTSE tracker fund. Unlike the fund manager who is trying to outperform a particular benchmark (most don't succeed over long periods), the tracker merely follows or matches a particular index as closely as possible.

Trackers fall into two broad categories, index funds and exchange traded funds (ETFs). For lower overall trading costs and ease of use, the simple OEIC (or unit trust) index fund will get the job done in most situations.

As mentioned earlier, it is important to maintain a well diversified portfolio. Global low cost tracker funds are an ideal way to do this.

The biggest providers of low cost trackers and possibly most popular are Vanguard and BlackRock iShares, who between them have $11 trillion of assets under management. Some other providers include HSBC, Fidelity, Legal & General and State Street.

A Model Passive Portfolio

As an example of how the above allocation could be covered by index trackers, I have set out a possible model portfolio including the current charges for each fund:

50% Global Equities

Vanguard FTSE Developed World ETF (charges 0.18%)

25% UK Gilts

Vanguard UK Government Bond (charges 0.15%)

15% Corporate Bonds

Ishares Corporate Bond (Ex Financials) ETF (charges 0.20%)

10% Global Property

Blackrock Global Property D fund (charges 0.23%)

(**NB** Charges will change from time to time but were correct at the time of publication)

The above portfolio options would have an overall charge of around 0.50% including typical platform charges. This would be a likely saving of at least 1% to 1.5% per year compared to the average managed personal pension fund. For a £50,000 fund, this represents a saving of £500 - £750 every year, which remains in your fund and will result in many thousands of pounds extra in your pot after, say, 30 or 40 years.

N.B. With some providers, there is no charge for the regular purchase of funds so in the above example you would substitute the ETF for the equivalent OEIC fund.

Simpler Options

Rather than selecting several index funds which will need to be rebalanced and adjusted for asset allocation as time passes, it will be worth considering a very simple strategy and look at the Vanguard multi-asset options.

The first and simplest would be their **Target Retirement funds**. Each fund has a target date - 2025, 2030, 2035 etc. and the investor simple selects the year from which they intend to start retirement.

These funds have been available in the USA for many years and used in the UK by some company pension schemes but has not been widely available to retail investors until their launch in 2016. The fund's annual charges are 0.24% and therefore offer a cost effective, simple option for the 'buy-and-forget' sipp investor.

Each fund contains a blend of Vanguard's global equity and bond funds/ETFs which are frequently rebalanced to maintain the appropriate mix for the remaining period to the retirement target date.

In the early years to mid 40s (20+ years to retirement), the funds are 80% global equities and 20% bonds (similar to the LifeStrategy80 fund). Thereafter the portfolio gradually reduces the equity percentage and increases the bonds so that at age 68 years the mix is 50:50 then by age 75 yrs the equities are reduced to 30% and the bonds are 70%.

So, find a platform which offers these funds, choose your appropriate fund which matches your target retirement date, set up your DD for monthly contributions - job done!

Another simple alternative is one of the Vanguard blended **LifeStrategy** options - these offer various levels of equity/bond balance in a single fund e.g. LS60 provides an all-in-one fund comprising 60% global equity and 40% bonds with ongoing annual charges of 0.22%. For longer term pension investing of 15 or more years, I would suggest a higher equity exposure such as LS80 - 80% equity might provide better returns but this will involve more volatility which some people may find uncomfortable. Therefore each person must make their own decision on this and what level of risk/volatility they feel happy with.

There are many other funds which offer a similar option for investors. Some others I have looked at recently and worthy of consideration are Legal & General Multi Index and HSBC Global Strategy funds.

I have used these Vanguard options as the basis for my book **'DIY Simple Investing'** as they offer low cost, globally diversified, automatically rebalanced solutions which are simple to understand and implement.

One further point, whilst building your pension pot, you will need to reinvest any dividends. The easiest and most cost efficient way to do this is to purchase 'accumulation' units (rather than 'income'). Using this option, any dividends are automatically reinvested and this will be reflected in the pricing of the units.

For further reading on passive investing
http://monevator.com/category/investing/passive-investing-investing/

Active Investing

For those who may like a more 'hands on' approach, it is perfectly possible to adopt a more active style of investing but it is unlikely to be as cost efficient as the passive option.

In my book '**DIY Income**', I set out a step-by-step approach to using a combination of investment trusts and other collectives to generate income. This could be easily adapted to use as the basis for building the pension pot.

Many brokers offer a low cost regular monthly investing option - with YouInvest it is £1.50 per trade so this can be very economical way to buy shares and trusts or ETFs as long as your monthly contributions are sufficiently large to make it viable. For example, if you are buying in tranches of £500, the execution cost works out at 0.30% but with smaller contributions of say £100 p.m., the buying costs would be 1.5% which is probably not a good idea. It may therefore be necessary to accumulate several months worth of contributions and combine them with the tax credits to make a trade economical.

<u>With individual shares for example, once purchased, there should be no other costs involved except for the reinvesting of dividends from time to time.</u>

With investment trusts, the average annual charges range from 0.4% to 1% (plus any performance fees). Using an active approach, it should be possible to keep total charges below, say 1.0% overall. This may not seem a great deal and should certainly be cheaper than a managed fund however, it will probably be at least 0.5% higher than using the passive low cost tracker method. If you were to invest £200 per month for 30 years, this extra 0.5% would mean the difference of a total fund worth £179,000 with lower charges and £164,000 with 1% charges - a difference of £15,000 (over 40 years the difference would be £40,000).

Some people may be more familiar with open ended investment companies (OEICS) and unit trusts rather than investment trusts. In the past, these OEICS traditionally levied charges of around 1.5% which included a 0.5% commission which would be paid to the adviser or introducer for the duration of the pension. This would put them on a par with the managed pension fund. However, with the introduction of RDR from 2014, payment of commission has been banned and it is now more common to purchase a 'trail free' version of the fund with charges of around 0.50% - 1.25%.

There are undoubtedly some very good fund managers out there who may have beaten their benchmark over several years. The problem is, how do you pick the 1 out of 10 who will outperform the market in the future and also, how do you know they will remain as manager over the long term and can you be satisfied the extra charges will get you a better return over 30 or 40 years?

So, active or passive? The debate has been going on for many years and each person has to decide which method is best for them. For me, low cost trackers were not available when I was attempting to build my retirement fund. If I were starting out today, I'm sure the overarching consideration would be cost and for that reason, I would choose the low cost passive route. Having said that, I may well add a few investment trusts.

For further reading around this subject, I have posted a few articles on my blog website. One article relates to investment trusts and one relates to a blended index option :

www.diyinvestoruk.blogspot.co.uk/2013/04/investing-for-income-part-2.html (investment trusts)

www.diyinvestoruk.blogspot.co.uk/2015/04/vanguard-lifestrategy-one-stop-solution.html (Vanguard LifeStrategy)

One area where a managed fund is possibly more likely to deliver better long term returns is smaller companies. If you decide to include this sector as part of your asset allocation, it will therefore be worthwhile considering a managed fund or investment trust. The charges tend to be a little higher, generally between 0.75% and 1.25%p.a. but some have delivered outstanding returns over the past 10 years.

For example, I have held Aberforth Smaller Companies in my SIPP for many years. Average share price total return over the 5 years to end 2017 has been 16% p.a.

So, to conclude, it doesn't have to be an 'either/or' decision - you could choose a mixture of passive and active. A common strategy could be a core/satellite approach i.e. a core portfolio of passive trackers or Vanguard Target Retirement/LifeStrategy which would comprise maybe 70% or 80% of your total portfolio and possibly some investment trusts to add extra diversity.

The beauty of the SIPP is that each one can be exactly tailored to match the holders investment style, attitude to risk, allocation and size of fund.

8. Annuities and Income/Flexi-Drawdown

So, you've been building your retirement pot for many years, you have built a nice pension nest egg and the time has come to think about retirement. What's the next step?

Annuity

The traditional option when a person reached retirement age was to purchase an annuity. Notwithstanding the pension freedom changes introduced in 2015 (see below), an annuity may still be a good choice for some people.

An annuity is a contract between you and the insurance company. In return for the capital built up in your pension pot, the annuity provider will pay you an agreed sum of money, usually paid monthly, for the rest of your life. The choice to take an annuity is a one-off decision and when implemented it cannot usually be reversed.

Most people do not usually bother to (or realise they can) shop around, but accept the annuity offered by their pension provider. My advice to anyone is always shop around to see if you can get a better rate elsewhere. This is a legal right and is known as **'open market option'**. The difference between the rate offered by your provider for a £100,000 pension pot, and the best rate on the open market could be as much as £1,000 per year - for the rest of your life!

There are a number of types of annuity - flat rate, single life/joint life, guaranteed payment for 5 or 10 years, escalating (rising) by a fixed percentage every year or inflation linked.

The flat rate, single life annuity usually offers the highest starting annual income, however it will never increase so the longer you live, the more it will be eroded by inflation. The escalating or inflation linked annuity will provide an increasing sum each year, but the starting amount will be considerably less than the flat rate - typically 30% or so lower.

People aged 60 or over with a relatively small pension pot under £30,000 (increased from £18,000) have the option to take the lot as a lump sum payment rather than purchase an annuity. This is called **trivial commutation**. Provided you haven't already started taking a pension, the 25% is taken tax-free as with any pension, but the remainder of the payment is taxable for the year in which it is taken - for most people this will be 20%.

The other thing to be aware of is health issues. If you are a smoker and/or obese and therefore statistically likely to die at an earlier age, you will probably be entitled to an enhanced annuity i.e. higher than the average person with no health issues. Likewise, if you have a medical condition which reduces life expectancy such as heart problems, cancer or diabetes, you may be entitled to an impaired life annuity which again is higher than a normal annuity.

Annuity rates were traditionally lower for women as they live longer than men however, under a recently implemented European directive, insurance companies can no longer discriminate. Therefore men have been offered slightly higher rates and women slightly lower rates since 2013.

Annuity rates have fallen considerably in recent years. A pension pot of £100,000 in the mid 1990s would have secured an annuity of around £13,000 per year for the average man aged 65. By 2007, this had fallen to £7,500 and in 2016 it is on average £5,400. Also bear in mind these amounts will be taxable so there could be a further 20% tax to be deducted. There are few signs that rates are likely to improve in the foreseeable future.

Of course, annuities are only one of several options available. The other main choices are **income/flexi drawdown** and **taxable lump sum** (or uncrystallised lump sum).

Income/Flexi Drawdown

Opting for income drawdown instead of taking an annuity, means you can take an income from your pension pot which remains invested with potential to grow. When you take the drawdown option, you can still take the 25% tax-free lump sum just as with an annuity. Also, you can merely take the 25% lump sum and not draw any income at all.

The big difference between drawdown and the annuity is the uncertainty factor - with income drawdown, you take the risk of your pot not delivering the expected income, also the possibility of your capital falling during a prolonged market downturn and, of course, future governments moving the goalposts on pensions. The choice is not therefore clear cut and everyone must weigh up all the factors and make up their own mind.

Every sipp drawdown provider will impose charges for administration. As there are now many more providers, these fees have come down over the past 15 years or so. It is obviously worth establishing the level of these fees before selecting your sipp provider as they do vary.

The maximum sum which could be withdrawn was traditionally limited - but this has now changed from April 2015. You were permitted (from March 2014) to take a maximum of 150% of the single life annuity of someone of the same age and sex as laid down by the GAD tables. This was reviewed every 3 years.

As a result of the falling annuity rates in recent years, more people have been looking at income drawdown as an alternative.

Both flexible and capped drawdown have now been rendered largely redundant and be replaced by the changes under the new pension freedom provisions. They will however remain as an option for those who started to take drawdown benefits prior to April 2015.

Pension Benefits after April 2015

A significant change in pension rules means **from April 2015** a retiree can now draw their entire pension in one go, if they wish. For some, this freedom will mean retirement planning that can better suit their needs.

The changes will affect those aged 55 and over who have savings in a defined contribution (DC) pension scheme, such as a personal pension or sipp. In a DC scheme, the pension depends on the amount of money you, and perhaps your employer, have saved in the scheme. The changes do not apply to defined benefit schemes which are common in the public sector (final salary pensions).

Those who have a defined benefit or 'final salary' scheme will need to transfer out to take advantage of the new pension freedom and will need to seek financial advice if the scheme is worth over £30,000. The immediate access to cash can be tempting but anyone considering such a move should take a long hard look at all the benefits they would be giving up. In many cases, all that is achieved is to bring forward some cash flow at the expense of longer term income.

Prior to the changes, any money withdrawn above the 25% tax-free limit had been punitively taxed at 55% so most people would either purchase an annuity or convert to income drawdown.

There are now just two forms of drawdown - **flexi-access drawdown** and **capped or taxable lump sum (TLS)**.

Flexi-access drawdown is similar to the capped or income drawdown it replaced - you can take the 25% TFLS on the whole of your pension pot. The remainder stays invested and can be used to provide a regular monthly income or, if you do not require regular payments, you can request ad hoc payments as and when required.

In both cases, your annual allowance - the amount you are subsequently allowed to pay into a pension pot - falls from

£40,000 to £4,000. This is unlikely to be an issue for most ordinary retirees who cease pension contributions on retirement.

Now these changes have come into force, everyone has the option to withdraw whatever sum is appropriate over and above the 25% tax free lump sum and only pay tax at their marginal tax rate. For some with taxable income under £11,850 (2018/19) this will be 0% however for most the effective tax rate will be at 20%.

Capped

With the taxable lump sum option, your pension pot becomes something akin to a savings account and you dip in to withdraw a lump sum as and when required. For each withdrawal, the first 25% of the amount is tax free and the remainder is taxable. Your pension provider will make additional charges for each withdrawal so this needs to be considered as these admin charges will erode the remaining capital.

These changes mean that someone with a pension pot of £60,000 could elect to take the 25% tax-free lump sum (as before) and then immediately withdraw the remaining £45,000 which would be taxed as income for that year or it could be used to purchase an annuity (as before) or it could remain invested and some of the remaining capital and/or investment income withdrawn.

So, from April 2015, there is no cap on the amount of money that savers can withdraw from this arrangement, so income can be varied to stay within the basic rate tax or even nil-rate threshold for the year if desired.

Although these changes introduce more flexibility, they also mean that pensioners will need to exercise more responsibility in relation to what could be a large and tempting sum of easily accessible cash sum. Undoubtedly the temptation for some will be to 'have a ball' but for most, having carefully saved for 40 years or more, the choice will remain between an annuity and some form of continued investment for the longer term.

Be aware that pension payments will be taxed on a month 1 basis by your pension provider until such time as they receive a tax coding from HMRC.

In the following chapter, I will look at the mechanics of running a diy income drawdown portfolio based upon my personal experience of operating this for my own retirement income and suggesting ways to operate a sustainable income strategy.

You can always opt for drawdown and still take an annuity at a later date when rates may be more favourable. Alternatively with a larger pension, you could take an annuity with part of your pot to cover essential expenses and convert the remainder to flexi-drawdown.

Unlike an annuity, which is given up in return for an agreed income, the pension pot remains your property on death and will pass to your beneficiaries. If you die before the age of 75 yrs, the pension pot can now be passed on free of tax. Die after the age of 75 yrs and they can elect to continue to receive the income or can cash it in subject to a tax charge at the recipients marginal rate (previously 45%).

Pensions are typically held in trust outside your estate and so in most cases are free of inheritance tax (IHT).

Pensionwise

To help those approaching retirement to understand the recent changes to pensions, the government have set up the Pensionwise website and this will be the first point of reference for many. In addition to the info on their website, it will be possible to get telephone guidance via the Pensions Advisory Service or arrange an appointment with a pensions adviser at a local Citizens Advice office.

www.pensionwise.gov.uk

Finally, just a **word of caution to all - there will be a multitude of scammers and criminal fraudsters out there preying on the vulnerable, naïve and trusting individual pensioners. They will use many clever ways to part people from their pension pots. The industry forecasts indicate there will inevitably be many, many people losing huge amounts of money so please make sure you are not one of the casualties!**

The government are planning to introduce a ban on cold calling by June 2018.

9. Managing Income Drawdown

For those people who choose either not to take an annuity or who wish to delay taking it to a later date, and who choose not to withdraw the total pension pot, I will take a closer look at some of the broader aspects of taking income from the drawdown portfolio.

In many respects, it is very similar to running an investment portfolio within a stocks and shares ISA.

In June 2012, I converted my own sipp to income drawdown. I investigated the option of taking an annuity - the flat rate option would start at a slightly higher income than I could generate with drawdown - but, of course, it would never increase and its value would be eroded by inflation.

To compare like with like, the quote for an annuity escalating at 3% p.a. offered around 15% less income for starters and, in my opinion, would never catch up. Therefore, the option of income drawdown using 60% equities allocation to provide a steadily growing stream of income to keep pace with inflation was the better choice.

In 2015 following the changes which introduced pension freedoms, I converted from income (capped) drawdown to flexi-access drawdown which means I now have the option to withdraw as much or as little as I require from my pension.

Whereas previously I was limited by the GAD rules which restricted the amounts I could withdraw each year - roughly around 5% of my total pension pot, now I can request whatever amount I require for the coming year, indeed I could choose to take out the whole pot (subject to tax) - there are no limits.

In practice, it would not generally be a good idea to take out more than 4% or 5% each year as there would be a high risk of depleting the fund too quickly which would be unsustainable longer term.

The first thing to point out is that when you decide to take benefits from your pension, you always have the option to take 25% as a tax-free lump sum. This can be invested in an ISA to generate additional income if needed. The limits for a stocks & shares ISA for 2017/18 rises to £20,000.

From April 2015, as we have seen above, these previous withdrawal limits have been made far more flexible and it will be for each person to decide for themselves the level of income to be withdrawn from their personal pot.

There are two main strategies for obtaining income. One is to hold a portfolio of higher yielding equities and bonds or fixed income securities and to withdraw the **natural income** generated by such a portfolio.

The other would be to maintain a portfolio which is not necessarily geared towards higher income and to **sell off capital units** representing a proportion of the portfolio each year to provide the 'income' required.

Lets take a look at these two options -:

A) Natural Yield

If you have been building your pension pot with a passive strategy using low cost trackers, you may be unfamiliar with a change of emphasis from the build phase of growth to the benefits phase of taking income. One way to get more of a feel to the new approach is to gradually start to introduce the income producing securities into your portfolio prior to retirement. The income generated will, of course be reinvested so the portfolio will still be growing but you should get a better understanding of whether income drawdown is a viable option for you.

You will therefore need to re-evaluate the whole portfolio and possibly make adjustments to move from growth and/or reinvestment of dividends to a strategy that can generate a rising income stream which can be sustained into the future. As income will start to be withdrawn when benefits are taken, the rate of growth of the pension pot will reduce compared to when dividends were being reinvested. Also, you are no longer adding your monthly pension contributions.

Sustainable Income Levels

The obvious thing to point out is that you need to be confident your portfolio can generate the required income selected for a sustained period. If, for example your remaining pension pot is £100,000, and your portfolio was likely to generate a natural income yield of around 4.0%, this would be £4,000. Therefore, unless you deliberately choose to deplete capital, your sustainable income drawdown would need to be below £333 per month.

The second aspect to point out is that once your pension is converted to drawdown, it would be unusual to make any further contributions in the future. Therefore if capital is depleted year after year as a result of taking out more than the total returns from your investment fund, the level of sustainable income will rapidly decline.

If you will be relying on the income to cover essential living expenses in retirement, it is advisable to build a cushion representing 2 or 3 years worth of cash reserves either in your drawdown pot or elsewhere to cover any period when income does not arrive as expected.

Thereafter, calculate the income likely to be delivered by your portfolio over the coming year and then set your drawdown at, say 10% below this figure. Repeat the following year and then you should have a good feel for managing your drawdown income fund and what level of withdrawal feels comfortable and sustainable.

Until 2006, it was not possible to continue with income drawdown past the age of 75, at which time it was compulsory to purchase an annuity. This has now changed and drawdown can continue indefinitely.

Although the use of passive index funds are a good choice during the build phase, currently there are not too many options available for generating a natural higher income. This is a fast growing industry and this situation may well change over the next few years.

One option I have used for my own drawdown strategy has been the tried and tested mix of managed investment trusts.

Using Investment Trusts

With my own drawdown pension, I have found that a balance of 60% equity and 40% bonds and fixed interest securities will get the job done for me.

The equities consist of a variety of investment trusts selected from mainly UK and global income sectors and UK Property/Infrastructure sections. In addition, some of the trusts focussed on Asia and the Far East can add diversity and also have a reasonable yield. If you have been using income orientated investment trusts as part of your portfolio during the build phase, these can remain during the benefits drawdown phase. The only difference will be that the income they provide will be withdrawn rather than reinvested.

I find that trusts can provide a smoother, more predictable income stream than funds as they can hold back some excess income in good years and pay it out in poor years. Most established trusts in the income sectors will typically hold between 12 and 24 months income reserves.

Funds (OEICS) on the other hand, are obliged to distribute all income received and the revenue will fluctuate from year to year which is obviously not ideal. For further research I recommend The Association of Investment Companies (www.theaic.co.uk) and also Trustnet (www.trustnet.com/investment-trusts)

In addition, there are many large FTSE companies which have paid solidly rising dividends for many years and these could also be used to generate drawdown income as part of your portfolio. Companies such as Shell Oil, Vodafone, GlaxoSmithKline and Unilever are large FTSE 100 constituents - sometimes referred to as blue chips - and have been producing growing revenues and profits over many years. These are the sort of companies which have weathered the storm following the global credit crunch of 2008 and have also managed to maintain a steady stream of rising dividends despite the severe economic downturn.

Investors who feel comfortable using individual shares and can cope with the additional volatility can use such a strategy to generate an income which is higher than the average for the FTSE 100. The process would be briefly, to identify around 20 large cap companies from different sectors of the FTSE 100 (and upper reaches of the FTSE 250). They should have good fundamentals - in particular, a strong record of rising dividends over at least the past 10 years; dividends covered at least 2x by earnings, a strong and rising level of free cash flow combined with low levels of gearing (borrowing). It is not necessary for each constituent to have a high yield but the overall average should be above the average for the FTSE 100 as a whole (otherwise you might just as well buy a FTSE 100 tracker!).

Personally, I prefer collectives to individual shares when dealing with my pension as they are more diverse and less volatile.

My book **'DIY Income'** goes into some detail and provides a step-by-step guide to generating income using a mixture of investment trusts and individual shares.

For further ideas and possible research in this area I recommend some of the articles on my blog '**diy investor (uk)**' www.diyinvestoruk.blogspot.co.uk .

If, however, you decide to use a variety of investment trusts from the UK income sector, you will find they all hold most of these larger, higher yielding companies so for simplicity, I would probably suggest sticking purely to the ITs.

Some trusts which have done well for me over many years include City of London, Finsbury Growth & Income and Temple Bar. I provide these merely as an example and not a recommendation and, of course, each person must carry out their own research.

Some other options to investment trusts might include Vanguard UK Equity Income Fund which holds around 130 shares from the FTSE 350 and with charges of 0.22% and their global income fund All World High Yield ETF (VHYL) with charges of 0.29% however, as previously mentioned, the flow of income from funds and ETFs is not so predictable.

Bonds & Fixed Income

So far as fixed income is concerned, I believe it is advisable hold a diverse selection. This could include such securities as retail bonds and preference shares.

You could look at higher yielding corporate bonds via investment trusts or ETF providers like Blackrock iShares. At certain points in the cycle it will also be appropriate to look at gilts and inflation linked gilts.

With a combination of well chosen fixed interest securities, it should be possible to obtain a solid return in the region of (currently) 3% to 5% or so without too much difficulty. The interest on gilts, and corporate bonds is paid gross and as they are held within a sipp there is no tax to pay.

The easiest way for the average SIPP holder to gain access to this sector will be via fixed income collectives - either investment trusts or funds as they will hold many different securities which helps to spread the risk. The average charges for such collectives are between 0.75% and 1.25% p.a.

Another option could be the multi-asset funds which hold a blend of different assets all in one fund. I guess the popular choices for many fairly cautious income seekers would be the 20 - 60% equity sector funds.

The small reservation I have with these types of funds is that the fund manager has the freedom to increase or reduce exposure to various classes of asset according to how they see market conditions - the returns for investors will therefore depend upon whether the manager can make consistently good calls

Again, these are not a recommendation but given as an example of the areas to consider when you undertake research in this area (assuming you decide to hold fixed interest securities).

The advantage of a proportion of the portfolio being held in fixed interest is firstly the possibility of a higher yield over equities depending on the selection and also that future income payments are usually a known quantity, unlike dividends from equities, which may be held flat or reduced in times of low profitability. This makes bonds ideal for people who wish to secure future income over a defined period of time.

They add a degree of solidity and certainty to the income stream.

For more research in this area as well as some interesting articles - http://www.fixedincomeinvestments.org.uk/fixed-interest-blog

B) Sell off Investments for 'Income'

There may be lots of people who have, for many years, operated an auto-build sipp by dripping monthly contributions into low cost index funds.

If I were starting out in my 20s or 30s today, this would probably be central to my investing strategy for the longer term. These may well be a variety of globally diverse and balanced index funds or ETFs which provide a good return but which may not generate a decent natural income.

Switching from this to an unfamiliar income strategy outlined above may be a little daunting and appear complex - for many it may be unnecessary as it is always an option to maintain the investment strategy that has served the investor so well over possibly many years.

At the point of retirement, the contributions will cease, however, the underlying funds and investments will continue to grow. The average long-term growth for a globally diverse, balanced fund of equities and bonds may be in the region of 4%, 5% or 6% per year after adjusting for inflation.

There is no real difference between taking 4.0% 'income' from a fund which generates an average total return of ~5.0% by selling units to selecting higher yielding investments with a natural yield or distribution of 4.0% but where the total return is equally ~5.0%.

For those invested in index funds, it should therefore be a relatively simple process to sell some of the accumulation units, say at a fixed point each year.

The level of sell off will be for each person to decide but for those looking to stay within the safe rate of withdrawal zone, it should be possible to take out say 3% - 4% at the end of each year for 'income' and this should be replaced by the growth in the investments over the coming year.

For those deciding to use such a strategy, it will be prudent to have some form of cash buffer covering 2 or 3 years 'income'. This can be used to provide income in bear market years when returns on the investment fund may be negative.

On a practical note, the annual sum withdrawn can be placed in a savings account and monthly withdrawals made to cover day-to-day living expenses.

Safe Withdrawal Rate

We are all living longer - so goes the mantra - but we don't know how long we will live - some will live to 100, some will die in their 60s or 70s. The big danger for many people will be running down their pension pot too quickly, especially if they have been dipping into capital for unplanned expenditure.

It will therefore be important to have some sort of plan or strategy to take advantage of the new pension freedoms. The key question will be - what is the safe and sustainable rate of withdrawal? For many years various academic studies pointed to a rate of 4% but more recently other studies suggest a reduced figure may be required to take account of lower returns and longer life expectancy.

The traditional goal of wealth accumulation is generally to seek the highest returns possible in order to maximise wealth, subject to the investor's risk tolerance. After retiring, however, the fundamental objective is to sustain a certain standard of living while spending down assets over an unknown, but finite, length of time.

Investing <u>during</u> retirement is a rather different matter from investing <u>for</u> retirement, as retirees worry less about maximising risk-adjusted returns and more about ensuring that their assets can support their spending and lifestyle for the remainder of their lives.

Of course, you would probably want to hold those investments which generated the higher returns - so equities would be in the mix as they provide higher returns than bonds or cash deposits (over the long term). Fixed interest securities, as the name suggests, will not do this (but they may give some modest capital appreciation). However some bonds and fixed interest securities such as corporate bonds and gilts are less volatile and will provide a 'smoother' ride.

So, getting back to the basic question - what is a sustainable longer term drawdown rate? It will depend upon a number of factors

Some Questions to Consider

What level of income do you need in retirement?

What is the timeframe? Check out average life expectancy for age/gender.
http://visual.ons.gov.uk/how-long-will-my-pension-need-to-last/

Personality type and attitude to risk?

What will the balance between equities, bonds and other assets in the mix?

Natural Yield or Total Return approach?

Do you want to exhaust the pot or leave a legacy?

What other income will you receive - state/company pension, Buy-To-Let rental, inheritance etc?

What Level of Drawdown is Sustainable?

First of all to clarify, we are talking about taking a certain level of income from the investment pot which can go on indefinitely with very little possibility of the pot being exhausted regardless of future market conditions.

Various studies have suggested that a rate of 4% should do the job.

This was the figure suggested by Bengen in 1994. His studies showed that a 4% rate would have been successful in any 30 year period from 1926.

The 4% figure was later confirmed by the Trinity study which showed that a 4% withdrawal using 50/50 equity/bond allocation over a 30 yr period was successful 100% of the time.

https://www.bogleheads.org/wiki/Safe_withdrawal_rates#Trinity_Study:

However, more recently, other research has suggested this figure is too high. For example, Wade Pfau suggests that in today's low interest rate environment future returns on equities and bonds are likely to be lower and therefore a more realistic rate of 3% should be used.
.
http://www.fa-mag.com/news/why-4--could-fail-22881.html?section=47

The McKinsey report suggests returns for the 30 years to 2014 may have been exceptional and that we should expect significantly lower returns from both equities and bonds over the coming 20 years.

http://www.mckinsey.com/industries/private-equity-and-principal-investors/our-insights/why-investors-may-need-to-lower-their-sights

Most of the research I have seen is based on returns from the US market. However there is a recent study for the UK market produced for Morningstar which suggests that whilst historic returns for equities and bonds of the UK are broadly similar to global returns, for the near-term future they can be expected to be lower. The study also suggests a 50/50 balanced portfolio is most suitable for UK retirees.

http://media.morningstar.com/uk%5CMEDIA%5CResearch_paper%5CUK_Safe_Withdrawal_Rates_ForRetirees.pdf

It will be for each person to weigh up all the information and form a view. Personally, I find 4% has worked for me but others may prefer the more conservative 3% in the early years and see how it goes.

Drawdown Methods

There are basically three approaches:

Constant dollar/pound - in year 1 you draw say 4% of the pot (3% or 3.5% for the more conservative). In year 2 your withdrawal amount is based not on the value of the portfolio but upon yr 1 amount plus inflation. In subsequent years your withdrawal is based upon the previous year and adjusted for inflation.

For example, with a portfolio of £100,000 you draw £4,000 in year 1. The following year, you draw £4,080 and in year 3 you draw £4,161 (inflation 2%).

Regardless of the ups and downs of the market, income withdrawn will always maintain real spending power as it keeps pace with inflation. However, how would you feel taking ever increasing amounts whilst your capital is falling during a multi-year bear market?

Secondly **Constant percentage** - simply settle on a percentage figure, 3%, 4% or 5% and withdraw this percentage from your pot each year. Of course, the value of the pot will move up or down each year so the amount withdrawn will vary. This may not be an issue if the income is mainly for discretionary spending items and you have other income streams such as state pension for essentials.

Finally **Natural Yield** - you spend only the dividends and interest generated from your portfolio. This is the method I chose at the start of my drawdown phase using a selection of investment trusts and fixed interest securities.

Personally, I would feel more comfortable with a reasonably predictable annual income which will gently rise to keep pace with inflation. Therefore a combination of method 1 & 3 with the added flexibility provided by a 10% cash buffer.

The use of a buffer zone allows me to avoid selling a portion of my portfolio when prices are down. Working on the assumption that there is mean reversion in market returns, I hope this strategy will help to mitigate the effects of bear markets. It acts in a similar way to investment trusts use of dividend reserves which can smooth the distributions.

Much will depend on timeframe and asset allocation. For those working on a period of 10 years, it could well be possible to withdraw maybe 5% or 6% p.a. without doing too much damage to capital. However, longer term 25+ years, it may probably make more sense to start off with the lower figure of 3% or 3.5%.

Whatever the starting figure, it can always be revised - raised or lowered - as time goes by and actual returns and expenditure become known rather than guessed.

When it comes to pension drawdown, much will depend upon individual circumstances. There is no one-size-fits-all solution.

Furthermore, there are no certainties - everything revolves around percentages and probability. How long will you live; what about market returns; what about cost of living and inflation; will you need a care home - if so for how long?

One big factor in the above scenarios is the level of the markets at your starting point. Obviously, if you were lucky/brave enough to start the drawdown in March 2009, your chances of success with a relatively higher withdrawal rate would be much improved compared to, say starting out some 18 months earlier.

Another factor is individual personality - some people are naturally more conservative/cautious than others. Some are more risk-averse and will feel more comfortable with a lower equity allocation and a correspondingly lower return. There are no right or wrong decisions. The person who has spent the past 30 or 40 years carefully building his/her slow and steady pension pot will have a good sense of risk tolerance and is unlikely to adopt a gung-ho strategy by starting with a 6% withdrawal rate for the 30 or 40 years of retirement.

Finally, be aware that the SWR academic research is mostly looking at a 100% success rate and is based on statistics which cover a worst case scenario. The 4% 'rule' would obviously appear more sustainable based upon a 90% probability of success.

Many investors running a diy drawdown portfolio will be familiar with the concept of 'living within your means' and during periods of market downturn will naturally be able to decrease spending on non-essentials. Incorporating variability into spending can increase the safe initial withdrawal rate significantly.

What Level of Income to Expect

Depending on the asset allocation for income between equities and bonds, we might therefore settle on a figure of 3.5% for a sustainable long term rate of return. Lets see what sort of lump sum pension pot would be needed to provide what level of income.

Starting with a modest pension pot of -

£20,000 - this would generate an annual income of £700 or £58 per month.

£50,000 would generate £1,750 or £146 pm

£100,000 will generate £3,500 or £292 pm, and

£250,000 will generate £8,750 or £729 per month

Some people may be surprised at how large a pot is required to generate a modest monthly amount. For those who are contemplating starting a pension savings plan - do not put it off too long!!

Finally, as the years pass in retirement, many people's attitude to risk/market volatility will change. Generally, they become more cautious and may want to reduce exposure to equities and increase the proportion of gilts, bonds and fixed interest element of their portfolio. One rule of thumb is to hold your age in bonds.

10. Pension or ISA?

Both are a form of savings vehicle and have their particular advantages and tax breaks. Obviously, for more wealthy people, it will be a benefit to take advantage of both. However, if you have to choose between the two, which is the better option?

I have looked at two calculations - saving £2,000 per year (grossed up to £2,500 by HMRC) into a pension for the basic rate tax-payer for a period of 30 years and secondly £2,000 p.a. saved into a stocks & shares ISA. The platform and fund charges are assumed the same for both at 0.5% and the rate of return on both is 6% p.a. (calculations via Candid Money)

At the end of the 30 yr period, the pension fund would be valued at £186,000 and the ISA would be valued at £149,500.

All other factors being equal, the tax credits on pension contributions will always provide a clear advantage for the pension savings. However, these savings cannot be touched until benefits are taken in later years and also the pension benefits, except the 25% tax-free lump sum, are always taxable.

The ISA pot could generate a gross tax-free income of £5,980 per year assuming a withdrawal rate of 4%.

The pension pot could generate £1,860 from the tax-free lump sum of £46,500 and an additional £5,580 taxable income from the remainder. Assuming a tax rate of 20% in retirement this would become £4,464 nett. Therefore a total nett income of £6,324 from the pension compared to £5,980 from the ISA.

Lets look at the for and against for each -:

Pension

++For++

The fund is locked away, the earliest you can access it is age 55yrs (57yrs from 2028)

You get tax relief on contributions at your highest rate, so more beneficial to higher rate tax-payers

Generally you can potentially save more each year in a pension (up to £40K) than an isa (up to £20K)

Pensions do not usually count for IHT purposes

Pensions are not taken into account should you ever need means tested benefits

-Against-

The fund is locked away, the earliest you can access it is age 55yrs

With the exception of the 25% tax-free lump sum, the benefits are taxable

Some managed pension funds can involve high charges which impact on returns

ISA

++For++

There are no tax breaks on the way in, but interest and returns on investments are tax-free

You can access the money at any time

ISAs can be inherited without penalty

They do not need to be declared on your tax returns

-Against-

You can freely access the money - it is tempting to dip in and you have to be very disciplined

You are limited in the amount you can put away every year (£20,000 from April 2017)

Some investment products levy high charges which limit returns

They will count as savings should you need to resort to means tested benefits

---
--

Weighing up all the pros and cons, I personally believe, on balance, pensions should probably take priority. Definitely if you are likely to be a higher rate tax payer during the build phase and then a standard rate tax payer when retired and drawing pension benefits.

Also a definite if you are in a company scheme and your employer is making some contribution. This is free money.

Thirdly, there is a distinct advantage to have tax breaks on the way in, yet be able to take up to 25% as a tax-free lump sum.

N.B. The introduction of the new Lifetime ISA from April 2017 makes the choice less clear cut.

Lifetime ISA (LISA)

Introduced in 2017 they are designed to encourage younger people to save.

Anyone between the ages of 18 and 40 yrs can save up to a maximum of £4,000 per annum in the new Lifetime ISA. For savings up to the age of 50 yrs, the government will add a 25% bonus i.e a max. of £1,000 at the end of each year.

Therefore someone contributing the maximum from their 18th birthday could save £128,000 by the age of 50 yrs and receive total bonuses of £32,000.

The money can be used towards the deposit for a first home worth up to £450,000 or can be saved as a nest egg for retirement and taken tax-free from the age of 60 yrs. Unlike pension savings, withdrawals can be taken at any time before 60 yrs subject to the loss of bonus and also a 5% charge.

Individuals will still have the option to choose between cash LISA or Stocks & Shares LISA.

11. End bit…

In conclusion, I have tried to provide a simple guide to hopefully remove some of the mystery and apparent complexity surrounding pensions. I suppose the main two points to get across are the importance of **starting to save early** and secondly, to **avoid high charges**.

This is a guide, not a blueprint to be slavishly copied. The emphasis has been on producing a sort of route map for the individual who wishes to take more responsibility for his/her financial future.

It cannot possible cover every possible option and I have tried to keep it simple to make it as accessible as possible to a wide audience.

I hope it will encourage the reader to feel a bit more confident, optimistic and empowered to pursue their own plans for the future.

Whilst I have attempted to outline a simple approach to investing which I hope many ordinary people could embrace, I also accept that it is by no means suitable for everyone as I hope I have made clear earlier in the book. If some people have reached this point and have come to the conclusion that the approach of DIY pensions is not for them, that is absolutely fine. **It is not the aim of this book to persuade anyone to invest on the stock market** - merely to provide information, options and the (dubious) benefit of my personal experience of what works for me as a small private investor.

As ever, always carry out your own research and take responsibility for your investment decisions. If you are in any doubt about any aspect of your pension plans or require clarification about anything you have read in this guide, you should consult your own financial adviser.

Keep it simple.

Good luck!

* Start early

* Join the company scheme if available

* If young, be prepared for any state pension from age 70 at the earliest

* Low charges good - high charges bad

* Diversify

* Consider a low cost SIPP option for a diy pension

* Consider income/flexi drawdown as an alternative to an annuity

* Finally, **KEEP IT SIMPLE!**

Copyright © 2018 John Edwards

Some useful websites

My blog
www.diyinvestoruk.blogspot.co.uk

Online Sipp Brokers
www.charles-stanley-direct.co.uk/Our_Services/SIPP/
www.youinvest.co.uk/SIPP
www.hl.co.uk/pensions
www.bestinvest.co.uk/sipp
www.alliancetrustsavings.co.uk/pensions/
www.tddirectinvesting.co.uk/choose-an-account/sipp/

Product Providers
www.ishares.com/uk/individual/en/index.page
www.vanguard.co.uk/uk/portal/home
www.etf.hsbc.com/
www.legalandgeneral.com/investments/products-and-funds/index-tracker/
www.spdrseurope.com/index.seam

Some Robo Advisors
www.nutmeg.com
https://www.moneyfarm.com/uk/pension/
https://uk.scalable.capital/sipp
https://www.evestor.co.uk/pension
https://www.ig.com/uk/investments/smart-portfolios

Research

www.dwp.gov.uk/gov/
www.pensionsadvisoryservice.org.uk/
www.digitallook.com
www.theaic.co.uk
www.trustnet.com
www.morningstar.co.uk
www.monevator.com
www.retirementinvestingtoday.com
www.candidmoney.com/default.aspx
www.fixedincomeinvestments.org.uk

Community
www.moneysavingexpert.com

Other
www.citywire.co.uk
www.thisismoney.co.uk

My other books

'DIY Introduction to Personal Finance'
'DIY Income'
'DIY Simple Investing'

Further Reading

'Smarter Investing' by Tim Hale
'Investing Demystified' by Lars Kroijer
'Little Book of Common Sense Investing' by Jack Bogle

build a portfolio
  % equities   ┌ UK
  % bonds   └ global

platform fee
ongoing annual charges

6) choosing SIPP provider
   - percentage fee
   - flat fee

SIPP
- government invests
- tax deductible

1) - SIPP ≠ ?
   - ISA

2) consolidate 2 pension
   transfer fees

3) traditional funds
   index funds   UK share = equities?
   shares + truth,
   investment trade funds
   exchange
   bonds

4) regular purchase?
   funds
   dealing close

5) regular or
   occ. investment

Printed in Great Britain
by Amazon